First edition: First printing

ISBN-13: 978-1534821798

SEAL

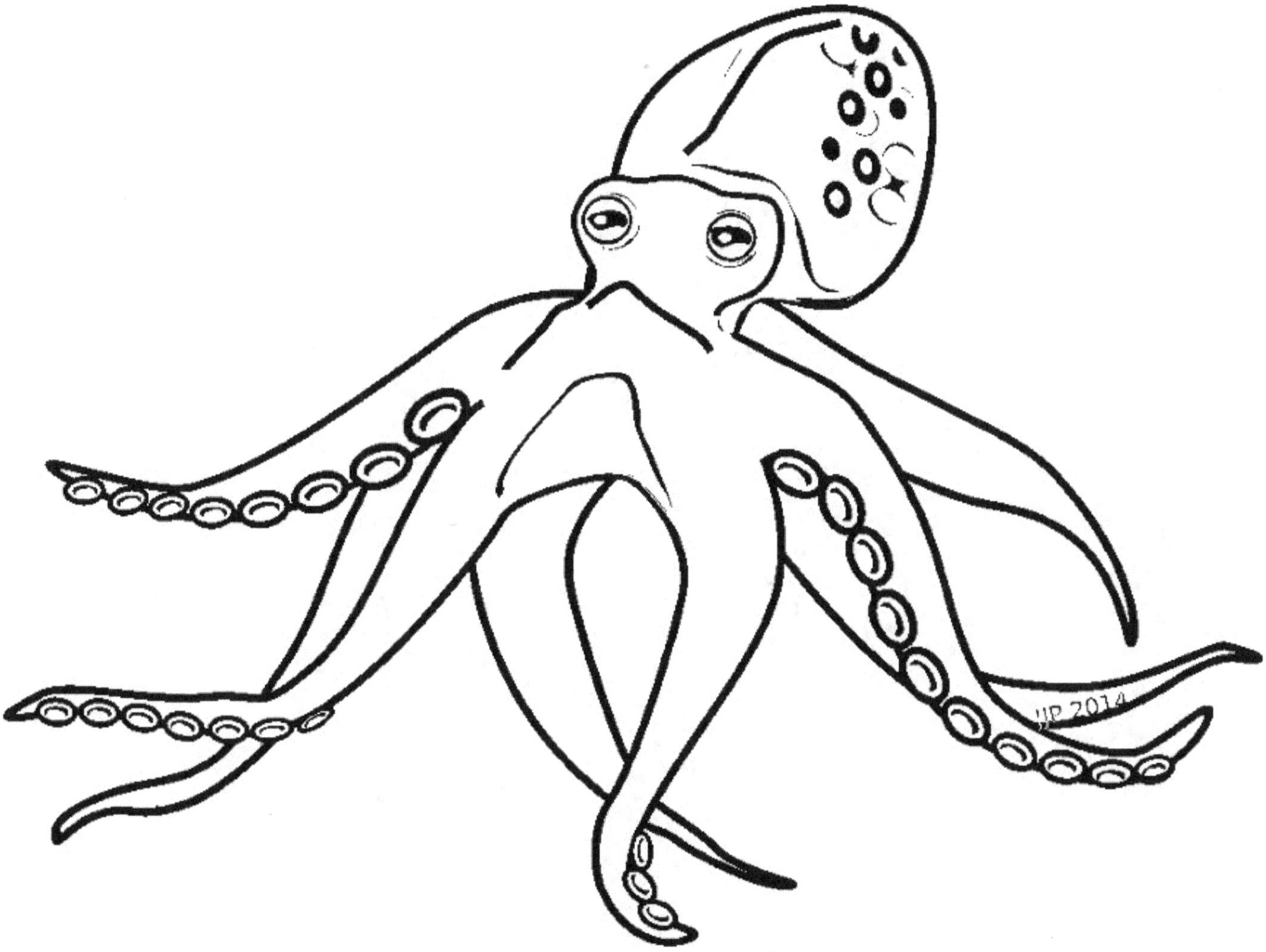

OCTOPUS

SEA TURTLE

CRAB

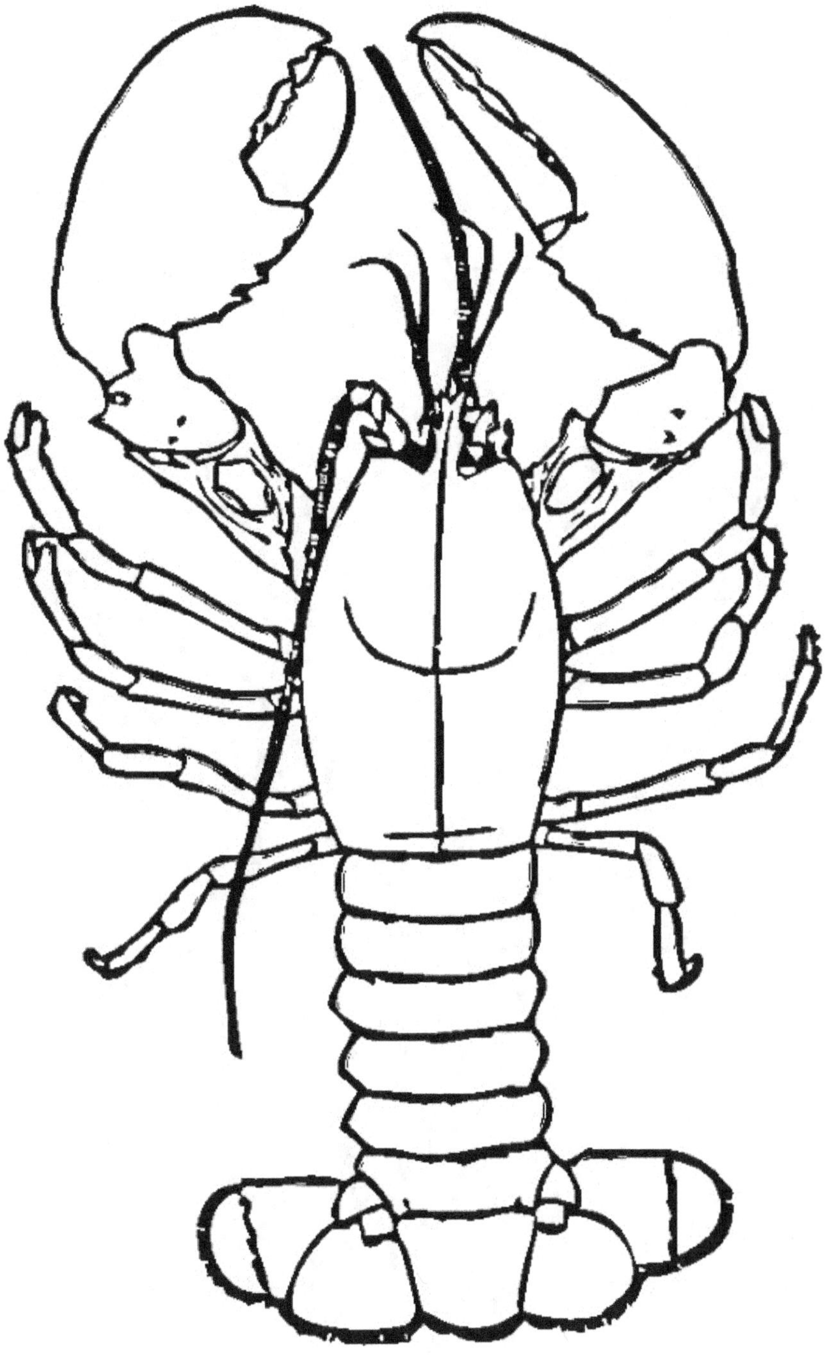

LOBSTER

DOLPHIN

OYSTER

JELLYFISH

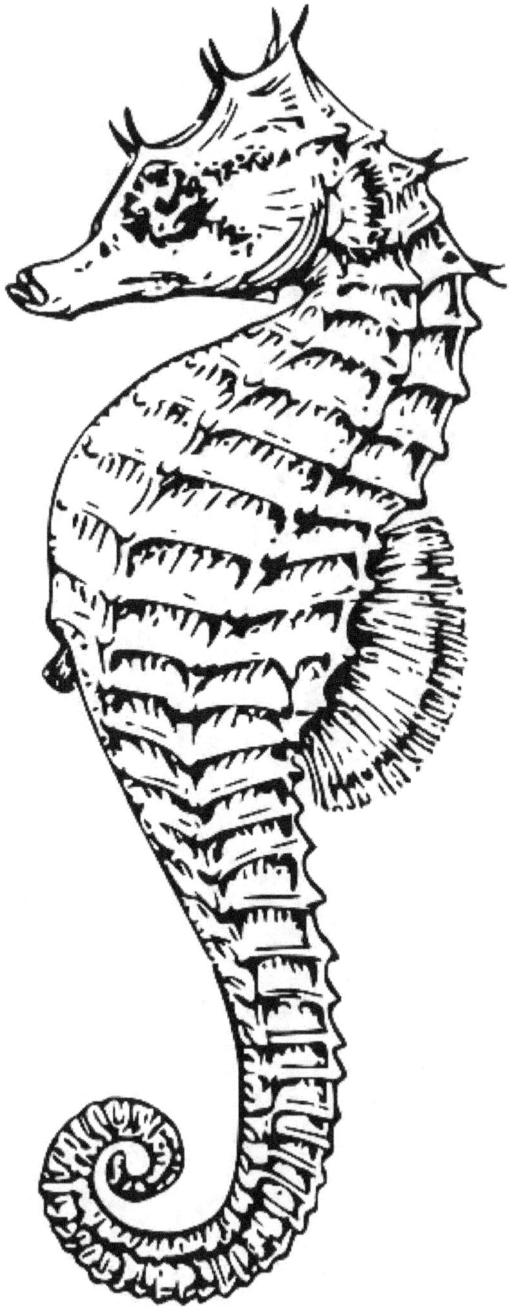

SEAHORSE

SHARK

STARFISH

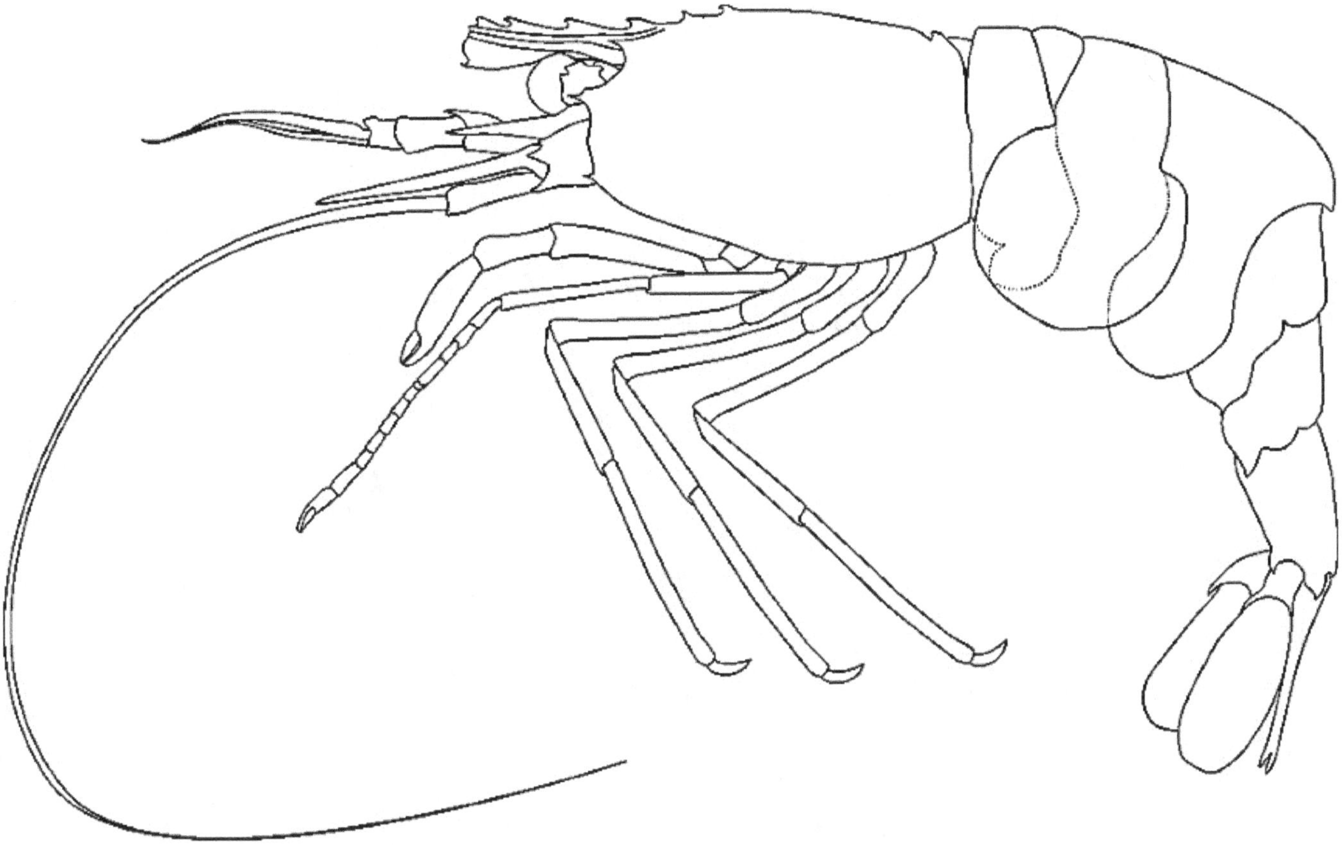

SHRIMP

WALRUS

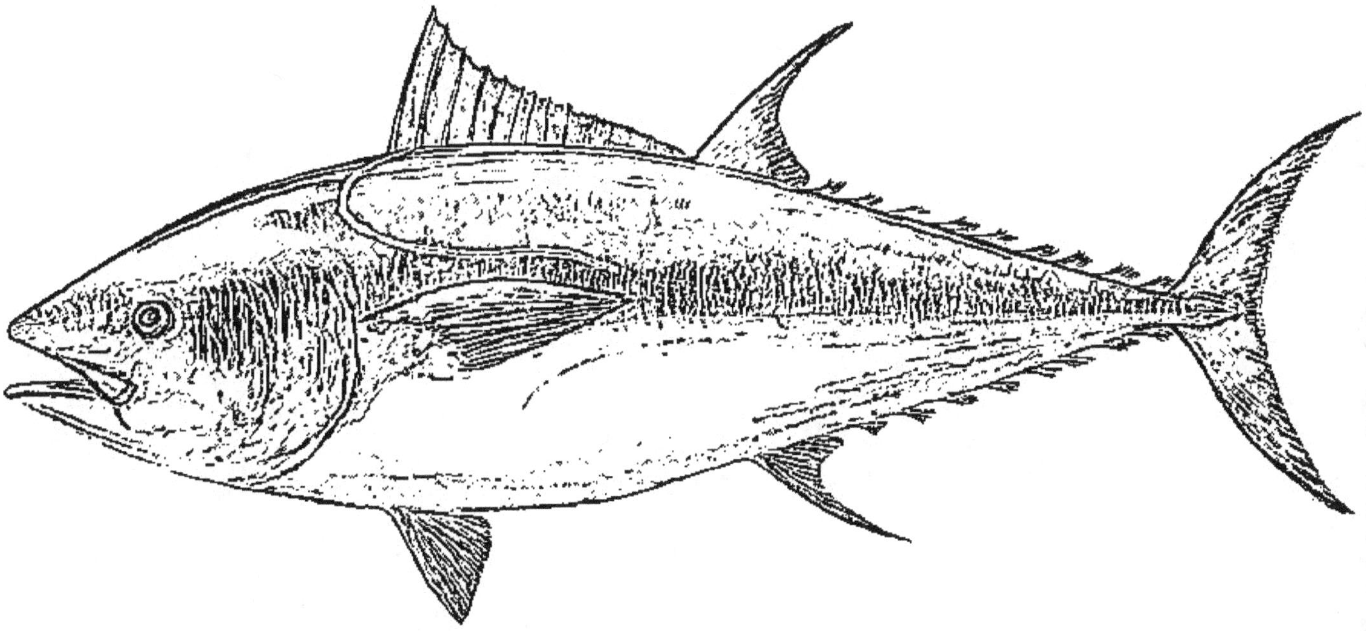

TUNA

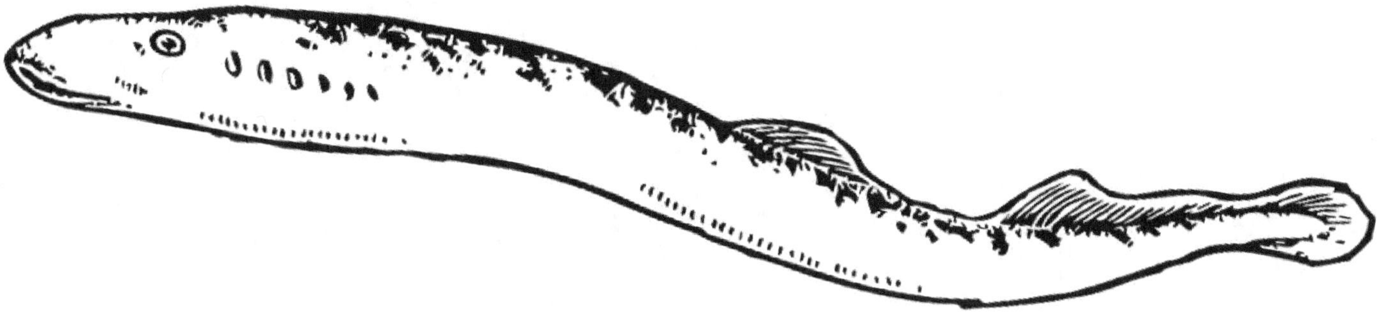

EEL

www.ingramcontent.com/pod-product-compliance
Lightning Source LLC
Chambersburg PA
CBHW081158280526
45787CB00008B/3377
* 9 7 8 1 5 3 4 8 2 1 7 9 8 *